Ink On Paper

tel

Ink On Paper

Copyright © by *tel*

All photos by *tel* unless otherwise indicated.

Library of Congress Cataloging-in-Publication Data

ISBN 978-0-9862213-2-3

Published by Pressing On Press, Inc.

First Printing June, 2017

First Edition

Printed in the United States of America

To Holly

so many reasons...

I have so many people I would like to Thank.

First and foremost my Grandma and Grandpa Salins. So many of my happy childhood memories are with them. They showed me unconditional love and what it means to be family. I miss you both every day.

Mrs. Miller, my high school summer school English teacher. You helped me breathe life to the writer inside.

My kids, Ronny, Ashley, Ally, and RJ. The four greatest loves of my life. You are all everything to me and encourage me to be a better person. There isn't a day that goes by that I am not proud and honored to be your Mom and to see the amazing individuals you have become.

My sister, Holly Salins Behning, Thick and thin we got through it together. Love you more than you know.

My Dad, Tony Salins and my Mom, Bonnie Salins. You have loved and supported me even in days I was too stubborn to see. I understand so much more now; more than I ever have.

Bob de la Mora, Jr., we have had some very steep mountains to climb, but we are doing it and will reach the top together with laughter, hope, and patience. Thanks for believing in me and in second chances.

My nephew, Levi, you are so talented and amazing. Love you so much.

To my family, cousins, aunts, uncles, all of you hold so many happy memories and love. Life gets away from us and we don't see each other enough, but you all mean the world to me.

My sisters and brother, Chris, Amy and Tim and their families. I am so glad to be a part of your family, love you guys.

To all my friends, each of you have a special place in my heart. Some of you are miles away, but always close in my thoughts. Thank you so much for being my friends and for memories old and new.

Art Kleck and Audrey Lewis, it is an honor to know you both, to call you friends, and fellow authors. Your styles and stories that you have shared, gave me the push I needed to begin this journey.

My Journey...

Ink On Paper

Old friend
Where have you been?
Pen to paper
Hello once again.
Many years have gone by
Yet you are right where
I left you.
Hello old friend
Where shall we begin?

Create
2013

tel

Leaves, Leaves
Oct. 1988

Geez Louise,

Look at all these leaves.

Floating around,

Not touching the ground.

Up in the air,

Over there.

Can't you see,

They're waving to me.

Leaves
2013

tel

Soft Kiss
Dec. 1988

Wild birds fly past me,

Whirling my hair.

In the misty, chilled air

I look up to see

Clouds forming your face.

I look down

Hearing birds

Singing our favorite song.

I start to run,

Stumbling,

I land at the tree

You carved our letters.

One last time,

I rise up

To feel

Your soft kiss

Upon my lips.

Honey
2002

tel

A tear fell from my eye

Not to shed in sorrow

But to glimmer in joy.

Point
2002

tel

Awakening

Dawn approaches

Longing to kiss rays

Upon sleepy buds.

Slight breeze,

Whispering softly

In the morning light.

Of promises

Only the stars

Knew of.

How I See
2012

tel

My Safety

Running through a field

of thorns

Trying to reach the shade

of my willow.

The safety of

its branches.

Hold me,

protect me,

From fears

of reality

That should only come

In nightmares.

Willow's Tears
2015

tel

Hiding

Where are my willow tree's branches hanging low

For who has cut them down?

Hiding spot of my dreams

Whispering in the winds.

Protect those who walked within

Looking for refuge

Among the bark of the reality.

Where are my willow tree's branches hanging low

For who has cut them down?

What harm could they bring

When all they have done is protect

A young girl's dreams.

Protection
2016

tel

Gray

Swirling of snow

Covering all life

Suffocating any hint of rebirth.

Too deep

For digging out

Can barely breathe.

Only from above

A light grasping to peek through

A glimmer of hope.

      No,

Only gray fading into dark

For now and possible for another day.

Snowy
2015

tel

Directions

Cold chill blows

Circling through the streets.

As the lonely walk,

Directions of the unknown.

Where does the heart guide you,

When your mind is so lost?

Where does the soul sing,

When the tune has faded away?

Cold chill blows

Circling through the streets.

As the lonely walk

Searching for a path unknown.

Path Unknown
2012

tel

For Me to Succeed

With his guiding hand

And a loving touch

I will succeed.

Support and excitement

In his eyes

Will take me further

Than my dreams.

Mountain Away
2002

tel

Sisters

Distance
> has come to us.

Never
> traveled away from another.

Even
> when life happens to,

Take
> new paths for each.

We
> were always close by.

Yet
> even as miles grow,

This
> bond won't be lost

For
> nothing can separate sisters.

Sisters
2014

tel

Pieces of You

A piece of you

Drifts past,

Away from me,

Where you've

Always been.

A piece of you

Traveling alone,

Away from pain

Where you've

Escaped from.

A piece of you

Remains here,

Inside my heart,

Where you'll

Always be.

My Aunt

unknown

If I Could Go Back

If I could go back,

   I would savor every moment with you

   I would spend more time listening to stories,

   Rather than telling them.

If I could go back,

   I would look deeper at you

  Memorize every image of time

  Hold your hand a little longer.

If I could go back,

   I would walk a little slower,

   Learn a little more

   I would take to heart the lessons you taught.

If I could go back,

   I would say I love you more

  Capture your light a little brighter

  Hug you a little longer.

If I could go back,

  I would hold you in my arms

 As I watch you go,

Whispering I love you.

Grandma, Grandpa & Me
1990

taken by Dad (Tony Salins)

R.A.A.R.

To discover within

A loss through time

Only to find answers

In my children's smiles

R.A.A.R.
2015

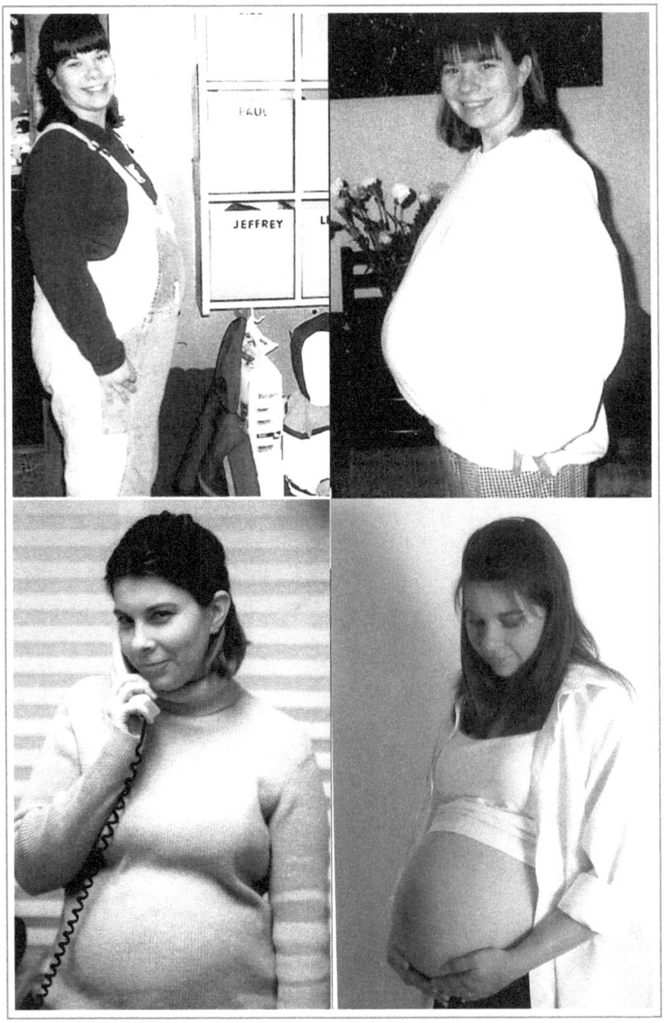

Unknown(top)/MORA Photo(bottom)

Moving Time

Time moving

Slowly

Pushing harder

For you.

Time moving

Rapidly

Growing away

From me.

White Flower
2013

tel

Little Sparrows

Little sparrows flying

In no direction known.

The wind carrying you along,

Away from the nest,

Adventures abroad.

Knowing not when you'll return

Old willow tree will weep,

But the wind will whisper

To you.

It won't forget,

The path home.

Ginny
2015

tel

Beginnings

Look in your eyes

Of love

and hope,

Gives me strength

and courage

To move forward.

A path anew

One less traveled.

Lights the way

To start our journey,

Towards new

Beginnings.

Moment of Beauty
2013

tel

Dreamed Again

Dreamed again

Just as all the others before

In front of your door

Barely knocking

You open

With a smile

As if you knew

Of my arrival before I had.

Falling into your arms

Catching me, lifting me up

As if I should reach the sky.

The world around us pauses

Letting the moment sink in.

Then eyes flutter as if

Too much light has gotten in.

Reality dawning,

Visions fading

Another one, like before.

Sunbeam
2015

tel

Fire

Warmth of lights' glow

Flickering and dancing

Around two,

As the embrace

Becomes one.

A Blaze
2016

tel

I once was plain

Until you made me

Beautiful

Beautiful
2007

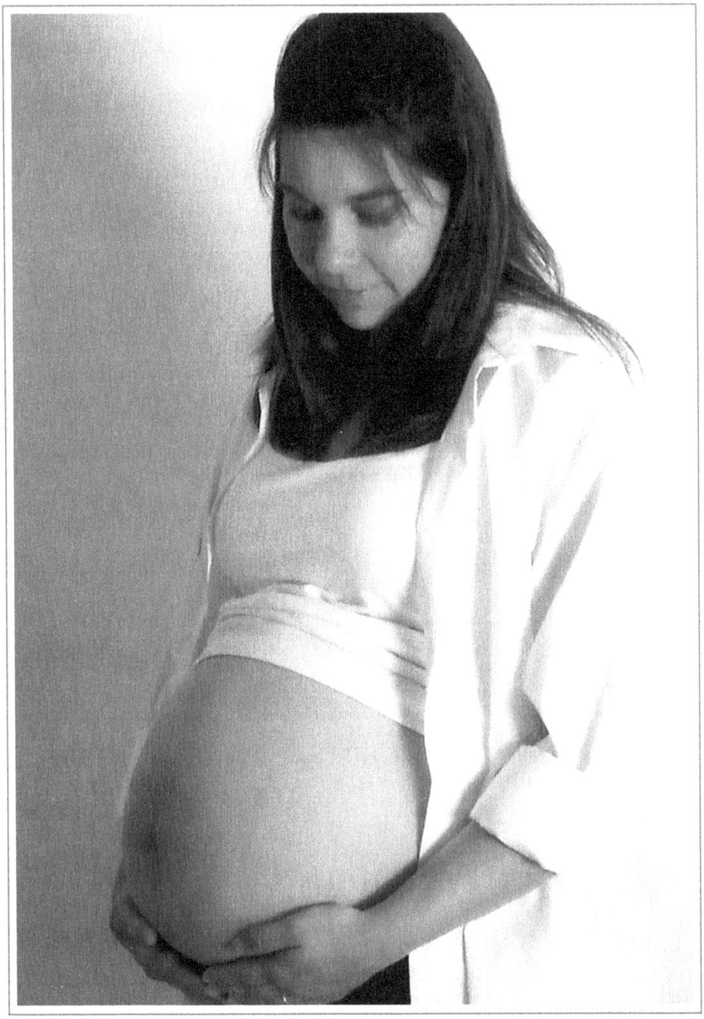

MORA *Photo*

Can Be

May have

Been shown

What love is not.

Only you

Have shown

What love can be.

Dew Drops
2016

AllyGab

I Shall

Guide me right,

I shall follow.

Take me higher,

I shall fly.

Love me always,

I shall forever.

Follow
2015

tel

Depths

Deep down

In depths below

Are answers hidden

Of questions

Too afraid

To ask aloud.

Long Way Down
2001

tel

No Sound

Laying in each other's arms

Not a sound made,

Yet millions of words are spoken.

Lasting
2016

tel

Made mistakes in the past,

In order to

Walk into the future.

Left Behind
2002

tel

In Search

Look out at the pond

Fog dripping rain

Have you traveled far

In search of the gray?

Trees bow their branches

In soak rained leaves

Have you drifted

In search of fallen hopes?

Flower petals graze

Your bare legs

Have you wandered

In search of joy?

Look out at the pond

Light starts to peek through

Have you stayed

In search of peace?

Wander
2002

tel

Forest Alone

I walked in the

Forest alone

Scared at the fact

You are gone

The warmth of your presence

Glows through

The darkness

Of our two worlds

Never to meet.

Though I feel abandon,

I am not alone.

I walked in the

Forest alone.

Slight brush

On my hand

Lets me know

You are with me, always.

Forest Escape
1998

tel

Rejected Advance

Late one night,

As time ticks by.

I want to journey

Into my dreams,

But they would rather

Glide across my pad.

Metal
2016

MORA Photo

My Disease

Body battered and worn

No answers, just unknowns.

Day to day life so hard,

Strains on ones being;

Withdrawn.

No explantation, no relief.

Failing, canceling, hiding.

Screaming within

Outward pushing on.

No relief to come,

Another day to start again.

Broken
2015

tel

Invisible

If you see me crying,
> I don't need your pity
>
> I need understanding.
>
> Warm embrace
>
> Makes me feel
>
> I can get through
>
> Those dark days.

If you see me smile,
> Don't think I am fine.
>
> I hide behind
>
> Several masks
>
> To shelter pain,
>
> A front from glaring eyes
>
> Judging, misconstruing.

If you see me crying,
> Don't ask why
>
> For in this moment
>
> Of time,
>
> What I need
>
> Is just one person to understand.

Peace
Blanchard, OK 2013

tel

Someday

Someday,

        Is just down the road.

Someday,

        Will turn into today,

Someday.

Along
2004

tel

Will You?

If I run to you,

    Will you wait?

If I shall fall,

    Will you catch me?

When I cry,

    Will you wipe my tears?

When I fall apart,

    Will you put me together?

Wisdom
2002

tel

You

Why do words

Allude me,

When you come near?

What hides behind

Those eyes,

When you look into mine?

Where do we go

From here,

When you reach for my hand?

The Walk
1999

tel

Second

A second in time

Can change

Your whole world.

How will you

Carry on?

Post
2003

tel

One More Race

Smell of burnt rubber

Transports her

Back to a time

That seems so long ago.

When a daughter and her dad

Shared those times

Special to them.

Watching from the stands,

She knows there is no better place

In the world to be,

Cheering on her dad.

Then just as fast as the cars

Speeding down the track,

Life takes some turns

To lead far away.

But in the distance she hears

Screeching of tires

Calling them back for

One more race.

Race
Thunder Valley Raceway Park, OK 2013

tel

Tokens

Rushing water

From a desert rain

Traps and claims,

Sand, stones, and things.

As fast as the

Rush of rain came

Sun evaporates away.

Leaving tokens of treasures

Until the next rain.

View
2001

tel

Pat Benatar...You Saved Us

With *Love Is A Battlefield*

Repeating on my cassette tape

I run listening to the lyrics,

Anything to take me away

From the pain,

 the sorrow,

  the rage.

It keeps us out 'til darkness falls

Only then

I can keep her safe.

Pebbles in line

 down

  to our rock.

Warnings we keep

So I can protect from this place.

'Til the day comes,

When we can walk away.

Safe
2015

tel

Looking Within

As time travels on

I look within to see

What has been keeping me.

From childhood dreams

To the woman longing for me,

Finding the answer came upon me one day.

For it was I who was never free,

Always doing for others

Giving up all of me,

As time travels on slowly.

I have learned within myself

I'll always rise

Making dreams come true

If I just believe

Then childhood dreams

Become a woman's reality.

Vegas
2000

tel

Our Walk

As time moves on I remember

The first time you walked with me.

Feeling a connection

Transported in time,

Of a past romantic lovers' stroll.

You reached out for my hand

Grasping ever so lightly,

As we began our walk

In life together.

Downtown
2014

tel

Night Sky

I see my dreams

Within the stars.

Forming from imagination

Blinking to reality

Goodnight World
2016

tel

Arch

The arch once formed

Crumpled apart

Ripping of one;

Two apart.

A balance of tranquility and turmoil,

Now on their own

Alone in territories

Forgotten unknown.

Fading out endlessly drifting,

Trying to make amends

Finding darkness

Breeds deep within.

The arch once formed

Balancing of one

Needing now to learn

To carry on; apart.

Arch
1999

tel

Bar Bends

I have discovered
    Walking in life,
Under cruel control
    Of some others' grasps;
Only leads you in circles
    Within a small cage
Gasping for air.
    However when one bar bends away
Being freed to discover,
    The strength which has been
Inside all that time.

Fallen Limbs
2002

tel

Tiptoeing

Looking in your eyes

I want to fall in.

Getting so lost in the depths

I won't come up for air.

As much as passion's desires

Wanting to explode.

I can't release all I feel from deep inside

Instead I choose to tiptoe

Towards our new horizons.

Enjoying every moment with you

Looking in your eyes.

Road to You
2002

tel

Mind's Eye

You drift into my mind

So unexpectedly.

Then moments pass,

Only to find

You've been thinking of me

Skyline
Chicago, 2016

tel

Upon the Door Step

Left a white rose

Upon the door step

Can you guess who?

Someone who cares

Ready to give all

And more.

Left a white rose

Upon the door step

Leaving a clue

Do you have a guess

Who it may be?

Left a white rose

Can you guess who?

Someone who wants

To love you

Now and always.

Floating
2012

tel

Knew Each Other

We already knew each other

Before we met.

I made different turns,

While yours went another.

Our paths may have crossed,

We stopped for a moment

But we missed each's glance.

Then one day,

-As time knew it would-

Our journey

Finally brought us together

And we knew each other

When we met.

Just a Look

unknown

Wish You Could See

You would have loved it here, I wish you could see
    All that I have started to discover
    Beyond city's flatlands
    Arriving to rolling hills tranquility.

You would be so proud, I wish you could see
    What I've started to learn
    Through roads that lead downhill,
    Then journey up
    Past all my horizons, I will be free.

I wish you could see, you would be smiling
    For all the hopes and dreams
    You wished for me
    Knowing I would be happy
    That are now becoming reality.

Ray of Hope
2016

tel

Each Day

Each day
> I fight
>
> The fatigue, numbness
>
> The pain, the stiffness

Each day
> "I am fine"
>
> My answer is
>
> To those who ask
>
> And for me to try and believe

Each day
> I fight
>
> Against my own body
>
> Making my days
>
> Unknown, good, bad
>
> Which weighs on guilt

Each day
> I hold on
>
> For someday
>
> Help will get me through
>
> Each day

Window To...
2016

tel

Blocked Out

Infant to teen,

    Child to adult.

What is carried over,

    What is seen?

How to remember?

    Once tucked away

Memories gone,

    Forever blocked out.

Abandoned
2014

tel

At Last

Run away
    Don't look back
    Pain,
It follows
    Ignore,
It vanishes
    Out of sight
    Hidden in shadows.
It creeps
    Away,
It loses
    Time
Its peace
    Look forward,
Its bright
    Light
Its free
    At last.

Down
2016

tel

Child

The heart beats

    Warmth filled dreams

    Sun shines brightly

My love flows for you

    Watching you grow

    Sends joy throughout

The heart beats

    With love for you

    Always.

Dad & Me
January, 1972

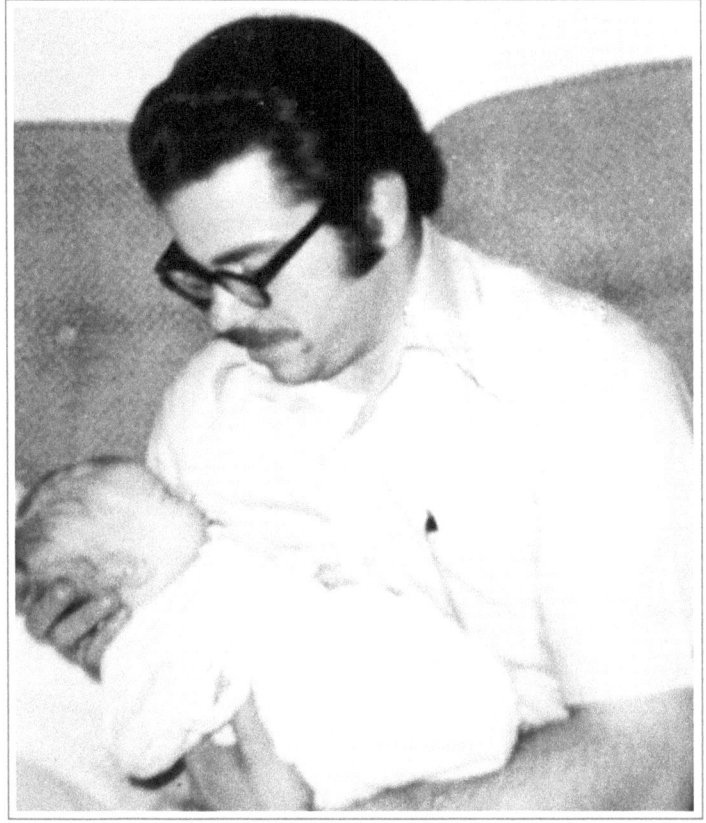

unknown

Your Power

Shine through
> A cloudy world
>
> To make life brighter
>
> When others see rain.

Shine through
> The darkness
>
> Bring hope
>
> When others lose theirs.

Shine through
> Bellows of smoke
>
> To clear the fog
>
> When others are blind

Shine through
> The depths
>
> Of dark waters
>
> When others gasp for air

Shine through
> A cloudy world
>
> To make life brighter
>
> When others see rain.

Sunshine on the Ground
2016

tel

Small Door

Small door

    Where do you lead?

    Curious the mind

    To what lies behind.

Small door

    What secrets do you hide?

    Tucked behind

    The key to questions forgotten.

Small door

    How long has it been?

    Since you

    Opened and invited us in.

Little Door
2001

tel

Journey

Path of gravel

Many twists and turns

 Ups

        and Downs.

In the journey of life

Seen you

     grow

         and change.

Always my little one

Even when

    You start on

        Your own journey alone.

Time
2016

tel

Inside

Wrote this

A hundred times

In my head

But it just seems

I can not

Bring it to paper.

Words swirl

Around,

Yet the pen is still.

Blank pages just stare

Back.

The want, the need

To tell

All the secrets

Trapped within

Is so strong.

So, I'll write it again

Inside my head.

Within
2002

tel

More to Come

Look forward

With bright eyes.

The past is behind you

The future is in your hands.

What adventures will you have;

Just wait and see.

Innocent
2010

tel

To Make

Letters form to make
    Words
Words form to make
    Sentences
Sentences make
    Paragraphs
Paragraphs turn to
    Chapters
Chapters create
    Books
Books open the
    World
        of
            Possibilities

Start A New Adventure
2016

tel

Memory

Bits and pieces

Cross through,

Like a small bubble

Just as it touches down,

POP!

They're lost again.

Bubble
2002

tel

Forgiveness

Forgiveness

To set you

Free.

Remember,

So it won't

Repeat.

Out There
2002

tel

Looming

Sleep escapes me

Where do I turn?

Dark shadows loom

Understanding is

Distance away.

Yet overhead

Vultures circle,

Waiting for

Life to die.

Soar
2002

tel

Once Knew

Swirling up towards

High clouds

See the light

Shining through,

Or is it

Your smile

Reminding me

Of things

I once knew.

Reflection
2002

tel

Brick Wall

Brick wall

Surrounds you.

Unyielding

Even Thor's hammer

Couldn't bring it down.

What caused the construction,

Life building

One brick at a time.

Wish you could break free,

Bring down the barrier

Allowing happiness, love

So you may enjoy life

Instead of hiding from it.

Meter's Out
2001

tel

Temper

Rage builds,

Like a roaring fire.

Smoldering spark

Soaring to towering flames,

No amount of water

Can extinguish the pulse.

Then as quickly as it ignites

Rage collapses

Into darken ash.

Ashes
2015

tel

Once Was

I am

But a shell of the woman

I once was.

The flame inside me

Been smothered out.

Lost in darkness and pain

Stolen from me,

An invisible assailant.

Lost in the sea of reality

Scrambling to reach the surface

Gasping for air.

I am

But a shell of a woman

I once knew.

Shell
2010

tel

Locked Eyes

Across the room

Faith plays her game,

Putting us in a moment

Stoping time and space

For us,

To look into

Each other's eyes.

Window to the Soul
2016

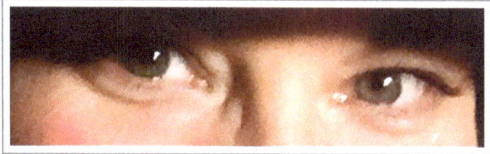

tel

Meadow Fields

Sun gently sets

Its tired rays down.

Memories of

The past disappear.

In the dawn

More cherished ones

Will appear.

Under
2014

tel

Moon's Reflect

Bare trees branches

Blow in cool night air.

Moon cast shadows

To dance and play

Upon the forest floor.

Light from above

Breaks through,

Enough to catch

Your shadow

Approaching me.

Birth
2002

tel

Locked In A Box

Deep inside,

Locked in a box

Tucked away

A special love.

For it has been

Damaged & drained,

Until one day

Someone will

Hold the key

Of trust, honesty,

True love, & faith.

Knowing secrets,

Strength, and power

To keep it safe

Unlocked.

Boxed Away
2016

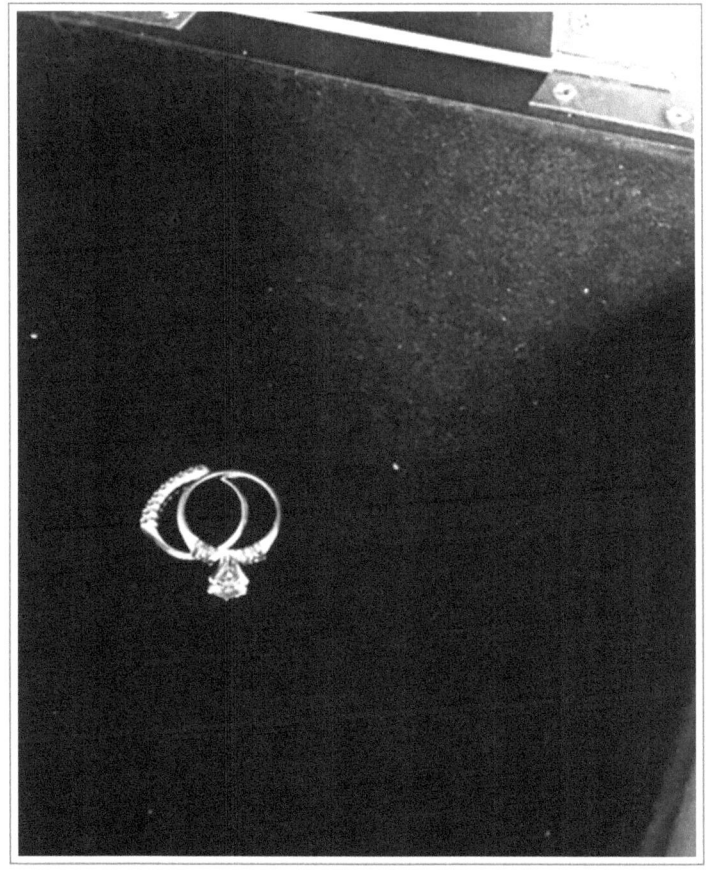

tel

Old Woman

Old woman looking out the window
What advice do you hold,
Could you share with me?

The stories you may have
Knowledge you must have grabbed,
Could you help me find my way?
With the wisdom of the years
What can I learn from you?
I know that I have had many downfalls,
You where there to help with the tears.
Now I am ready for what my life can bring
And how to finally be strong, even on days I feel weak.
Tell me the secrets hidden in your advice
Knowing that one day I would understand more than
I ever thought I could.

Old woman looking out the window
What advice do you hold,
Could you share with me?

Gate
2001

tel

Wandering

My mind wanders off

So many paths

unknown,

Yet amazingly

They all journey

Back to you.

All Aboard
2012

tel

Dreams

Turned around

To see

You standing

In front of me

As if

You have been

Waiting for me

All this time.

Bright
2015

tel

Fallen Tree

Tall and strong

How old are you?

What has grown

Around you?

Is it really important

To know?

When they have to destroy

Is it worth it?

For when it reveals your rings

With a crashing fall,

Then all is

Silent.

A shell left

Of once was

Tall and strong.

Age
2016

tel

Season's Welcome

Snow's first fall

Lays its tired head

Upon ground's bare hills;

As warmth aura

Shines through frosted windows.

Tree light glow

Fire's crackling music low,

Brings forth peace and joy

To once bustling year

Gone by.

All Is Bright
2015

tel

About the Author

tel

tel started writing during the summer of 1986. She met a teacher, Ms. Miller, who encouraged her to continue writing after seeing her work in her English summer class.

Since then she has written poetry and short stories, which she has only shared with a few family and friends.

In 1998, ***tel*** had two poems published in a local newspaper. This gave her the confidence to continue writing.

She lives with her family in a northern suburb of Chicago.

www.ingramcontent.com/pod-product-compliance
Lightning Source LLC
Chambersburg PA
CBHW041615220426
43670CB00004B/58